THE HISTORICAL CHARACTER OF ST. JOHN'S GOSPEL

THE HISTORICAL CHARACTER OF ST. JOHN'S GOSPEL

THREE LECTURES DELIVERED IN WESTMINSTER ABBEY
IN ADVENT, 1907

BY

J. ARMITAGE ROBINSON, D.D.

DEAN OF WESTMINSTER

WIPF & STOCK · Eugene, Oregon

Wipf and Stock Publishers
199 W 8th Ave, Suite 3
Eugene, OR 97401

The Historical Character of St. John's Gospel
Three Lectures Delivered in Westminster Abbey in Advent, 1907
By Robinson, J. Armitage
ISBN 13: 978-1-62032-670-1
Publication date 12/15/2012
Previously published by Longmans, Green, and Col, 1908

CONTENTS.

THE HISTORICAL CHARACTER OF ST. JOHN'S GOSPEL.

I.

OUR earliest account of the life and death of Jesus Christ makes no effort to define the nature of His person or to interpret His relation to the world's history. St. Mark offers us scene after scene in quick succession, with scarcely a single comment and with no desire to enforce a doctrine or a moral. The naturalness with which the story developes itself is due to mere faithfulness to the facts; the unity of the work is not the result of conscious art.

Two subsequent evangelists have made St. Mark's Gospel the basis of their fuller narratives. Each of them is in his way a literary artist: each has constantly in view the impression which his work will make upon his readers —Jewish or Gentile Christians, as the case may be. Each rearranges the materials he borrows from St. Mark, and modifies their phraseology with the view of enforcing certain principles or avoiding possible misconceptions. Each seeks to be in some sense an interpreter of the story, teliing it afresh for the greater edification of Christian believers. Yet this element of interpretation is strictly subordinate: the main purpose of each writer is that of historical narrative.

When we open the Fourth Gospel we are at once conscious of a different literary atmosphere. It is not a chronicle, but a study, of the life of Christ. The interpretative element is no longer subordinate; it is the dominating factor of the composition. The meaning and issue of Christ's work is the supreme interest: its relation to the whole history of humanity is considered at the outset; its effect on individuals and classes of individuals is traced at every step. All the way through the Christ presents Himself for acceptance or rejection; men are being judged —they pass judgment on themselves—by their very attitude towards Him. Belief or disbelief, and consequently life or death—this is the tremendous alternative. And the book is avowedly written, not to convey historical instruction, but to produce conviction: "These things have been written that ye may believe that Jesus is the Christ, the Son of God, and that believing ye may have life in His name" (xx. 31).

It is easy to exaggerate this interpretative element. We are, indeed, at the present time being seriously asked to suppose that the evangelist, eager to display his own conception of Christ's person and mission, and finding no sufficient illustration in the scenes which tradition offered, gave full play to his imagination and constructed situations, characters, and conversations to serve his didactic purpose. But this supposition loses sight of a consideration which ought to be always before us in dealing with the earliest documents of Christianity. The new religion proclaimed itself from the outset as the truth, in contrast to the falsity of heathen beliefs. "The truth as it is in Jesus;" "Truth came by Jesus Christ;" "Ye shall know the truth:" such is the key-note of the earliest teaching. It was the new facts that scattered the old heathen mythologies. It is to my mind impossible to doubt that the evangelist of the Fourth Gospel intended the scenes which he describes to be accepted as real occurrences; it is impossible to believe that he knew them all the while to be the outcome of his imagination.

I would not be supposed to mean that a writer fifty years after the events would not give a certain colour to the details of a picturesque narrative, and would not modify the expressions of a discourse or a conversation, so that the result should not be a literal reproduction of what we should have seen or heard had we been present. But it is one thing to recognize a strong personal element in the construction of a narrative, and especially of a narrative in which dialogue plays a large part; it is quite another thing to suppose that incidents have been created for the sake of the instruction they are to convey. We may admit that the element of interpretation has largely controlled the structure of the book, the choice and arrangement of materials, even the language attributed to speakers: we may admit that teaching which was only latent, and only recognized long after, has been made explicit by a writer who cannot always distinguish between what was actually uttered and what he believes was involved in his Master's words. But I for one cannot admit that the writer of the Fourth Gospel has knowingly offered us parable for fact, and has recorded with the most vivid and convincing realism scenes of Christ's life which he knew to be historically untrue.

If we could doubt of our author's own meaning, we have but to read the first words of his Epistle, which forms a kind of epilogue to his Gospel: "That which was from the beginning, which we have heard, which we have seen with our eyes, which we have looked upon and our hands have handled, of the Word of life . . . that which we have seen and heard declare we unto you."

These are the words of a man to whom facts have brought a revelation: not of one who conjures up imaginary scenes in order to clothe spiritual conceptions in an attractive form. I desire to recognize that the element of interpretation, which gradually enters into the narration of the Gospel, reaches its maximum in St. John; but I am not willing to exaggerate this element of interpretation so as to destroy the historical character of the events which it undertakes to interpret.

We may picture to ourselves a writer at the close of the apostolic age anxious to place on permanent record the fruits of his long experience, which has gradually revealed to him the meaning of the unique events of his early days, when he moved in company with Him whom now he knows as the eternal Word who became flesh and dwelt among us. Such a study of the life of Christ as he would write, an interpretation of His mission and its issue, composed with the express purpose of deepening conviction in Christians already familiar with the main facts and the principal figures of the history, might well be quite independent of earlier narratives. It might assume their general contents to be known, it might occasionally offer a silent correction of their order or their details, and it might largely supplement them by dwelling on incidents and teachings which they had omitted. This is,indeed, just what we find in St. John's Gospel. It is in the main a Gospel of *paralipomena,* of "lines left out," passages of our Lord's life unrecorded hitherto.

So then we pass on from speaking of the different literary atmosphere of which we are conscious when we turn from the Synoptists to St. John's Gospel, to say something of two other contrasts which immediately strike us—the difference in the character of the teaching attributed to our Lord, and the difference in the scenes of His ministerial work.

The swift and vigorous sketch of our Lord's life contained in St. Mark's Gospel presents so natural and so convincing a development of the historical situation, that we can readily understand that two subsequent evangelists should have accepted it as the necessary groundwork of their larger books; so that, notwithstanding some modifications and many additions, derived largely from a second source, the outline of the story as each of them tells it is practically the same as before. This Synoptic account, as it has for some time been named, impresses our imagination all the more because it seems to have a threefold attestation. In one sense, indeed, it has; for its acceptance by the two later writers is a testimony to the belief of the

Christian community in their day that St. Mark had, if incompletely, yet truthfully described the life of the Master. But the historian is bound to remember that we have not here three documents independent in origin and each confirmatory of the other two, but one document which has been adopted more or less fully by two subsequent writers. As he cannot suppose that either of these two writers was an eye-witness of the events which St. Mark records, he will generally prefer St. Mark's original statements to any modifications of them which they have introduced; and he will regard the Synoptic outline as ultimately representing one clear view by one well-informed narrator of a life of which much necessarily remains untold. The second important document which the first and third evangelists had in common, and which they used in very different ways to fill out St. Mark's brief outline, cannot now be reconstructed as a continuous narrative. But whatever its original form may have been, it is plain that the embodiment of large portions of it did not require in the judgment of either of them the abandonment of the general scheme of narrative which they had accepted from St. Mark. At any rate, neither of them so far varies from St. Mark as to narrate any ministry of Christ in Jerusalem until the last days before the crucifixion. This restriction is the more remarkable in view of the fact that the non-Marcan document contained the apostrophe to Jerusalem—"How often would I have gathered thy children, as a hen gathereth her chickens under her wings; and ye would not".

Here, then, is a problem which the historian has to face. His earliest document confines our Lord's ministry in the main to Galilee, and does not bring Him to Jerusalem at all until the last week. Two subsequent writers have accepted the general outline of the story in this respect, although they embody words from another document which *primâ facie* suggest frequent visits to Jerusalem. On the other hand there are two considerations to be weighed. It is unlikely in itself that Christ should have so far departed from religious usage as never to visit Jerusalem for any of the great feasts during the period of His public ministry in Galilee. It is also unlikely in itself that He should have neglected the religious centre of the nation, and made no appeal to it until the very close.

Does not the solution of this problem lie in the consideration that St. Mark's Gospel is Galilean in its interest, and accordingly restricted in its scope? Is it not easier to believe that visits to Jerusalem should have been left unrecorded by a narrator whose interests lay in

Galilee, than to suppose that such visits never were made? At this point of perplexity St. John's Gospel comes to our aid with a new historical fact. It informs us that besides the ministry in Galilee reported by St. Mark, and accepted as the basis of their narratives by the first and third evangelists, there was also a ministry to "Jews" in the narrower sense ("Judeans") in Jerusalem; that this ministry was not continuous, but intermittent, taken up from time to time as the great feasts came round; that its teaching was of a different character from that which was given to Galileans, and that the situation thereby created was wholly unlike that which arose out of the Galilean ministry.

The Galilean ministry, as described by St. Mark, opens with enthusiasm which ripens into an unbounded popularity. When opposition manifests itself, it is not native opposition, but the envious interference of religious teachers, who form part of a system which centres in Jerusalem, and who are sometimes expressly noted as coming from Jerusalem. The Jerusalem ministry, on the contrary, as described by St. John, never arouses enthusiasm. It has to do with those who challenge it from the outset. There is no atmosphere of simplicity and frankness to welcome the new manifestation of power and sympathy and liberty. The witness is delivered to a hostile audience, whether they will hear or no. Ultimate issues are quickly raised; for keen critics perceive at once the claims which underlie deeds and words, and the claims in consequence become explicit. The relation of the teacher to God is the vital interest. In Jerusalem this question must needs be raised at the outset, and must recur again and again. Upon the answer it received, and upon the reception of that answer, the crisis must turn.

From the Galilean standpoint the tragic close had been sufficiently accounted for in the simple narrative of St. Mark. Conflict with Pharisaic religion and disappointment of popular Messianic expectation had nullified the effect of the Galilean work. There was no movement in force, no wave of enthusiasm which could carry Jerusalem; and so Jerusalem proved fatal to a Messianic claimant whom it dreaded and disliked; it conveniently disowned Him and handed Him over as a discredited pretender to be executed by the Roman government. Here was the plain fact, and it was a sufficient reply to the natural questions of the first generation of Gentile converts, living at a distance from the scenes of the great events, and little acquainted with Palestinian Judaism. But the plain fact, thus simply related, left grave questions untouched. Why was Jerusalem so fatally hostile? Had it never been given a chance of knowing its Messiah except by hearsay? Had it never seen Him till the last week? Such is the impression left upon the reader of St. Mark's Gospel. Or was there a whole region of activity unnoticed by St. Mark's brief record? Had there been concurrently with the development of the Galilean situation another development unconcerned with Galilee, which would explain the decisive blow which was finally struck in Jerusalem?

That such a concurrent development was possible arises out of a peculiar phenomenon of Jewish religious life—out of the custom of attendance at the great feasts in Jerusalem. Here were the natural opportunities for periodic visits to the religious centre at its moments of highest activity. Now the crucial historical statement of the Fourth Gospel is this—that from feast to feast a mission went forward, never indeed welcomed, but persisted in with unflinching determination until that last passover which brought its final rejection. Broadly considered, this is historically probable.

These preliminary remarks will prepare us to recognize two ruling features which characterise the whole of the Fourth Gospel—it is interpretative and it is supplementary. It sets itself to interpret the meaning and scope of our Lord's mission; and it does this mainly through the medium of the hitherto unrecorded story of the repeated manifestation of His personality and power and the assertion of His claims, where of necessity they must have been most thoroughly canvassed, at the religious centre of the national life. It is a story of days long gone by, treasured in a loving memory, and illuminated by an experience which has gradually learned its inmost truth. It is a story told not by an historian, but by a spiritual teacher; explained and commented on at every point in the light of subsequent knowledge, till at times the narrative seems merged in the commentary, and we are in doubt whether the evangelist is even intending to record the words of another, or is speaking to us directly in his own person. The picture of the Christ which he draws for us is not simply the bare recollection of what met his untutored eyes in those far-off days, surprising and amazing, contradicting expectation, and waiting for the issue to interpret it; it is the full truth of what was then half-hidden, half-revealed, but is now plainly seen to have been the manifestation of the Divine glory in human flesh.

The prologue, or opening section of the Gospel, shows us that St. John's interest is more than historical, in the narrower sense of the word; it belongs rather to the philosophy of history.

It goes back for its starting-point behind human birth and lines of ancestry. It begins, like the first page of the Old Testament, "In the beginning". It connects the Christ with the eternal purpose of God. He is the creative Word, which God spake, and by which all things were made. He is the Life, and He is the Light of men. He became flesh, to declare to men the invisible God. The destiny of each man depends on his acceptance or rejection of the Light and Life thus offered to him. These first words place us at the point of view from which the evangelist writes. His Gospel is the story of the great rejection, written for the warning and the encouragement of such as have received and welcomed the Divine gift.

The mission of the Baptist is assumed to be familiar, and is commented on rather than narrated: "He came to bear witness of the Light, that through him all men might believe". But some new points are given us. In a figure which gathers up the lessons of the law and the prophets, the Baptist speaks of Jesus as the sin-bearing "Lamb of God". A few eager souls are thus prepared at the outset to recognize the Messiah, the Son of God, the King of Israel. But the meaning with which they used these current titles then was but the narrow national conception, which had to be painfully unlearned. For it was not as the Jewish Messiah, but as the Light and Life of men that He would be known and received.

The incidents which close the first chapter recall the brightness and simplicity of the Galilean story of St. Mark; and the figures that meet us are mainly Galilean. The second chapter actually takes us to Galilee. Hitherto the Lord has given no special sign of power or grace. His personality is itself gracious and convincing: it wins and retains the true-hearted disciples of John. The first sign, when it comes, is like no other miracle. It breathes the exquisite fragrance of the spring-time; it has all the geniality of the early Galilean ministry of the primitive Gospel. It supplies human deficiency and it sanctifies human joy. At the same time it offers a deeper lesson: it is a parable of the highest optimism—the enrichment of human life by an infusion of the Divine, man's water changing into God's wine.

In sharp contrast with this gentle Galilean scene stands the first visit to Jerusalem. At the time of its most sacred feast we see the temple crowded with greedy traffickers. The swift severity with which He avenges the insult to His Father's house reveals a new side of His character and of His power.

The reader of St. Mark's Gospel is surprised

to come so soon in the Fourth Gospel upon the cleansing of the temple, which he has learned to place in the last week of our Lord's life. But on reflection he observes that, whatever the exact date may have been, the relative position of the incident is the same in St. John as in St. Mark. In either Gospel it forms the first public act of the ministry in Jerusalem. If it does not find an earlier place in St. Mark, it is because that Gospel records but one visit to Jerusalem. And we may further note that in both Gospels this startling action is followed by a challenge to declare by what authority our Lord so acts; so that in Jerusalem the ultimate issue—His relation to God—is raised at the outset.

This marks the essential difference between the ministry in Galilee and that in Jerusalem, and it confirms us in thinking that St. John gives its rightful place to this incident. This violent scene is followed by the secret visit of a leading Pharisee. The same uncompromising sternness demands from the very representative of religious Judaism the completest change—a new birth. It is the sequel of the message of the Baptist—the axe is laid at the root of the tree. It is John's baptism raised to a higher power—water and spirit, as he had foretold. Reform is not enough; reconstitution only will avail.

Nothing could accord more closely with historic probability than the opening part of this conversation: "Except a man be born again he cannot see the kingdom of God". "The kingdom of God" is not a Johannine phrase. The short, sharp, parabolic utterance reminds us of sayings found in the Synoptic Gospels. Its very repetition is characteristic also. Compare, *e.g.*, St. Mark's, "How hardly shall they that have riches enter into the kingdom of God," followed up at once, when objected to, by "It is easier for a camel to go through a needle's eye, than for a rich man to enter into the kingdom of God". But in the closing words of this interview St. John passes imperceptibly from recording the language of the speaker into comment of his own. He marks the crisis which necessarily follows the manifestation of the new light: men are judged already by their attitude towards it.

When this beginning was made in Jerusalem the Baptist was still at his work. When Jesus retired into the country, men came to Him to be baptized, till He found Himself placed in a position of rivalry with John. John, indeed, recognized that his own work was closing; but Jesus withdrew from Judea altogether, and journeyed northwards. We cannot now pursue the history further, but this small section of it presents us with all the elements of contrast that mark off the Fourth Gospel from the Synoptists.

I wish, before concluding, to develop one point a little further. In considering the historic probability of the position which St. John assigns to the cleansing of the temple, we must recognize more fully than we are accustomed to recognize the influence of the Baptist's mission upon the opening of Christ's ministry.

In St. Mark the Baptist forms the starting-point of the Gospel; but we are expressly told that he was cast into prison before our Lord's Galilean work began. Yet even so, the brief summary of the message of Christ, with which the Galilean ministry opens (i. 15), includes the Baptist's demand of repentance as preparatory to the reception of a new manifestation of Divine power. This germ of connection is developed by St. Matthew, who makes the first preaching of Christ identical with the preaching of the Baptist—altering St. Mark at both points so as to give twice over the phrase, "Repent, for the kingdom of heaven is at hand" (iii. 2; iv. 17). Still, there is a deep meaning in the note that the Galilean ministry was not commenced till John's work was closed; and men marked the contrast between the sternness of the Baptist and our Lord's familiar intercourse with all classes.

Now for the first three chapters of the Fourth Gospel the historical position is different: the Baptist's mission is still in full career. We are especially reminded that "John was not yet cast into prison" (iii. 24). Jesus is even found at this period adopting John's method, and baptizing even more disciples than he—though the evangelist presently corrects himself by saying that Jesus did not Himself perform the rite. The whole question of purification by baptism was under discussion. The baptizer with water had already pointed to the baptizer with spirit (i. 34). He now declares, "He must increase, I must decrease". But Jesus will not allow of the invidious contrast, and when He hears of it departs altogether from the scene. Samaria is visited on the way to Galilee, and when the Lord returns to Jerusalem John's mission is spoken of in the past tense (v. 35): "Ye were willing for a season to rejoice in his light".

But that former visit to Jerusalem had as its background the great religious fact of the moment which was impressing all men's imagination—John's baptism of repentance in the wilderness. When Nicodemus was told, "Except a man be born of water and spirit he cannot enter the kingdom of God," he would necessarily be reminded of the Baptist's work and words: the whole of John's mission lies behind the saying. And so in the light of the Baptist's predictions of the axe laid at the root of the tree, and of the cleansing of the threshing-floor and burning of the chaff, the scene in the temple courts appears to match with the character of the time. It is as though the Lord were carrying into the city the work of John in the desert. We are familiar with the application of the prophecy of Malachi to the preparatory mission of the Baptist. May we not believe that the whole context of the words was in our Lord's mind that day? "Behold, I will send My messenger, and he shall prepare the way before Me, and the Lord whom ye seek shall suddenly come to His temple . . . but who may abide the day of His coming? . . . He is like a refiner's fire. . . . He shall purify the sons of Levi, and purge them as gold and silver". (Mal. iii. 1*ff.*)

It might well have happened that the fourth evangelist writing long afterwards, when greater events had thrown the Baptist's mission into the shade, might have done no more than recognize his early testimony to Christ. But it is not so. It fell to his lot to record a portion of our Lord's ministry which ran concurrently with the Baptist's career; and, both upon the surface and when we pierce beneath it, we find the signs of this concurrence, as on reflection we feel that we ought to expect them. Our sense of the historic character of his Gospel is enhanced by this consideration.

My task this afternoon has necessarily been an apologetic one, for the historical character of the Fourth Gospel has been very widely denied in recent times. I have said nothing of the question of its authorship, for I have had occasion previously to state my reasons for thinking that the traditional assignment of it to the apostle St. John is more likely to be true than any of the alternatives that have been proposed. The question of its general faithfulness to historic fact is more important than the question of its authorship. That it presents grave historical difficulties I recognize, but I plead for patience and for sympathy in dealing with them. Every one who has experience in studying history from original documents knows that he almost always finds irreconcilable differences between his best authorities. Life is large and many-sided, and we have but the impressions of limited observers to describe it to us, and their restricted views result in paradox and seeming contradiction. Why should we expect it to be otherwise with the Life of lives, which, view it as we may, passes our comprehension?

But after all the Gospel of St. John is the one book in the Bible which stands in least need of the apologist. It commends itself by its astonishing power to our intellects and to our hearts. Some of you may have known the experience of passing through the darkest gloom of almost universal doubt, when all that you had trusted in the past seemed reeling and unsteady; and then, it may be, the only part of the Bible that still seemed to speak to you was the fourteenth, fifteenth, sixteenth, and seventeenth chapters of St. John. There at least, however it came to be there, was something Divine; and the best that was in you took courage and responded to recognised truth.

In Archbishop Temple's *Life* there are some letters to his son at Oxford, in which he enters sympathetically into his various philosophic difficulties. From one of these I will quote a few sentences in conclusion. "I am obliged to confess," he says, "that from seventeen to five and twenty I indulged largely in such speculations. But I felt all along like a swimmer who sees no shore before him after long swimming, and at last allows himself to be picked up by a ship that seems to be going his way." And then, after a few more words, he adds: "My passing ship was St. John".

II.

We are so much accustomed to mark the contrast between the language attributed to our Lord in the Fourth Gospel and that attributed to Him in the Synoptic Gospels, and to recognize the likeness of the former to St. John's own phraseology in his First Epistle, that we hardly do justice to the close correspondence both in idea and in expression to the Synoptic type which is exhibited by many of the great sayings which St. John has recorded. One example came before us incidentally at the close of the former lecture. It is worth while to dwell upon it a little more in detail. Our Lord's words to Nicodemus, "Except a man be born again he cannot see the kingdom of God," were met by the objection, "How can a man be born when he is old?" Instead of withdrawing or softening the expression, Christ repeats it with a fresh emphasis: "Except a man be born of water and spirit, he cannot enter into the kingdom of God."

"The kingdom of God," as we have before

noticed, is not a Johannine phrase; it never occurs again in St. John's Gospel or Epistles. The phrases "to see," and "to enter into the kingdom of God," are both found in St. Mark. The emphatic repetition of the condition of entry into the kingdom of God has a striking parallel in St. Mark's Gospel (x. 23-25), "How hardly shall they that have riches enter into the kingdom of God. And the disciples marvelled at His words, but Jesus answered and said again to them, Children, how hard it is to enter into the kingdom of God; it is easier for a camel to go through a needle's eye than for a rich man to enter into the kingdom of God."

If the rich man must become poor, so the old must become young. The incident immediately preceding is the blessing of the little children. "Of such as these," He says, "is the kingdom of God. Verily I say unto you, whosoever shall not receive the kingdom of God as a little child, shall not enter therein" (x. 14, 15). Compare St. Matthew xviii. 3, "Except ye turn and become as the little children, ye shall not enter into the kingdom of heaven".

The fundamental change, "impossible with men, but not impossible with God," is no less inexorably demanded in the short, sharp sayings of the Fourth Gospel; though the figure is slightly modified, and words are introduced which become intelligible and appropriate when we remember that the baptism of John was the great outstanding religious event of the time. The difficult discourse which follows bears many traces of the characteristic language of the evangelist himself, and towards the close of it most commentators agree that he is practically addressing his readers in his own person. Yet in the early portion of it we must note the phrase "the Son of Man"—occurring only, as in the Synoptists, on our Lord's own lips: and the hardly veiled reference to His death is in harmony with the stress and peril of the Jerusalem ministry. It is natural that the fatal crisis should be nearer to His thoughts here than in Galilee: "for it cannot be," so He said, "that a prophet perish out of Jerusalem".

We may now pass on to the next visit to Jerusalem, which is described in the fifth chapter. As in Galilee, so in Jerusalem issue is joined with the Rabbinic party on the question of the sabbath day. It could not have been otherwise. Power and sympathy and liberty, as we have seen on a former occasion, are the keynotes of the self-manifestation of Christ in the early chapters of St. Mark's Gospel. It was because He would not allow His power and His sympathy to be hindered and hampered by religious conventions, however sacred they might be held to be, that He touched the leper in spite of the prohibiting regulation and healed the man with the withered hand in the synagogue on the sabbath. It was this second manifestation of His freedom from conventional restraints that stirred up the Pharisees even in Galilee to plot against His life. At Jerusalem such action was yet more immediately dangerous. After the cure of the impotent man we read, "The Jews persecuted Jesus because He had done these things on the sabbath". They even sought to kill Him, and He soon retired to Galilee again.

It is instructive to observe the nature of the reply which the Lord made when first He was challenged for this action. We have several examples in the Synoptic Gospels of the various methods by which our Lord justified His relation to the sabbath. Once He appealed to the Old Testament story of David giving the sacred shewbread to his hungry men, contravening the regulation in the interest of a reasonable mercy. Then He took higher ground, and proclaimed the principle that the sabbath was made for man's good; it was to be his servant, not his master; and He added the profound saying, "The Son of Man is Lord of the sabbath" (St. Mark ii. 24-28). Before He cured the man with the withered hand He asked those who were watching Him with suspicion, "Is it lawful to do good to a man on the sabbath, or to do him evil? to save a life, or to kill?" (iii. 4). Other sayings are familiar: "If ye had known what that meaneth, I will have mercy and not sacrifice, ye would not have condemned the guiltless" (St. Matt. xii. 7); "What man is there of you who shall have one sheep, and if it fall into a pit on the sabbath, will he not take hold of it and lift it out? How much, then, is a man better than a sheep?" (xii. 11, 12). And once again: "Hypocrites, doth not each of you on the sabbath loose his ox or his ass from the stall and lead it away to watering? And ought not this woman, being a daughter of Abraham, whom Satan hath bound, lo, these eighteen years, to be loosed from this bond on the day of the sabbath" (St. Luke xiii. 15, 16).

In these replies we have sometimes the presentation of a parallel case, and a direct *argumentum ad hominem*, as we say; and sometimes the enunciation of a profound principle, which tends to modify the whole character of the institution in question. The reply to the Jews in St. John's Gospel belongs to the latter class. It is brief, pregnant, mysterious: "My Father worketh even until now, and I work" (v. 17). The problem suggested by the scripture, "God rested on the seventh day," in face of the fact that God's work in upholding the material creation knew no interruption, was no new problem in the Jewish schools. What was new and startling was the claim of Christ to identify His action with the Divine. He lifted the issue on to a higher level, and once again in Jerusalem His relation to God was the point on which all was made to turn. "For this cause, therefore, the Jews sought the more to kill Him, because He had not only broken the sabbath, but had said also that God was His own Father, making Himself equal to God" (v. 18). So the sabbath question falls into the background, and the discourse which follows concerns the relation of the Son to the Father. It is, however, worthy to be noted that on a subsequent occasion, when this same miracle was again under discussion, our Lord made a reply of the kind of which we have so many examples in the other Gospels: "I have done one work, and ye all marvel. Moses gave you circumcision . . . and on the sabbath day ye circumcise a man. If a man receive circumcision on the sabbath, that the law of Moses may not be broken, are ye angry with Me that I made a man every whit whole on the sabbath day? Judge not according to appearance, but judge righteous judgment" (vii. 21-25).

We may now proceed to consider the historical character of the story of the raising of Lazarus. I confess that I am not able to understand why this particular narrative should be regarded as peculiarly difficult to reconcile with historical probability. It does not appear to me to differ in any essential point from the stories of the raising of the dead which are contained in the Synoptic Gospels. The somewhat longer period which elapsed between the moment of death and the moment of revival only implies that the ordinary processes of decay were suspended by the Divine providence which intended the return to life. Indeed our Lord first spoke of this temporary death as a sleep from which Lazarus should be awakened; only when His disciples misunderstood Him to mean a natural sleep, from which there would be a natural awakening without the need of any intervention on His part, did He say plainly, "Lazarus is dead". Vital action was suspended, only to be restored by His personal intervention; but the process of decay was also suspended with a view to that intervention. The language of our Lord is closely parallel to that which He used in reference to the daughter of Jairus, "The maiden is not dead, but sleepeth".

I do not now address myself to those who are unable to admit that any of the narratives of the raising of the dead can possibly be historically true. I am only saying that to those who do admit the possibility of such a Divine intervention the circumstances of the revival of Lazarus need not appear to present peculiar difficulties. And with this preface I go on to consider what are the grounds on which, even for such persons, the story of the raising of Lazarus has been said to be wanting in historical probability. The chief objections to it appear to be three: 1. There is no place for it in the framework of St. Mark's Gospel; 2. It is directly inconsistent with St. Mark's account of the events which led to the crucifixion; 3. If it had happened, St. Mark must have known of it and mentioned it.

1. With regard to the first objection, our former study has shown us that it is not reasonable to regard the brief and rapid sketch which St. Mark has given us as completely covering even the main activities of our Lord's life. We have already had to refuse to rule out the occasional visits to Jerusalem, and the ministry which was carried on intermittently at the great feasts, on the ground that St. Mark makes no reference to them. We have admitted that his framework is too narrow for what appear to be the probable facts. In regard to the particular period which we are now concerned with, I would have you observe the account which St.

Mark gives of our Lords' journey from Galilee to Jerusalem. In x. 1 we find Him leaving Galilee for "the regions of Judea and beyond the Jordan": in xi. 1 He is preparing to make the triumphal entry into Jerusalem. The whole of the intervening period contains but five distinct incidents, and occupies only fifty-two verses. We turn to St. Luke's Gospel and find that this period occupies no less than 400 verses. With a mass of further material at his disposal he has enlarged the record of the journey to Jerusalem, as the best method of finding room for incidents as to which St. Mark is silent. It is plain, therefore, that St. Mark's framework was too narrow; but St. Luke seems not to have had the means of rectifying it with definite certainty, and so he fitted in his materials as best he could without seriously disturbing it.

2. The second objection is much more serious, if it can be sustained. It appears to me to shape itself as follows. The Fourth Gospel represents the raising of Lazarus as the immediate cause which led to the arrest and condemnation and crucifixion of our Lord. The sensation which it produced was immense. Terrified and exasperated by the popular emotion which it aroused, the two leading parties of Jewish political and religious life—the Pharisees and the Sadducaic high-priestly party—combined their

forces for the moment to rid themselves of a dangerous antagonist. The interest which Lazarus himself aroused was so great that a design was entertained of putting him also to death as a disturbance to the public peace. It was on account of the fame of this miracle that the multitude went out from Jerusalem carrying palm-branches to meet the Lord and conduct Him with triumph into the Holy City. The Pharisees said to each other in despair, "Ye see that ye avail nothing; behold, the world is gone after Him". There is no more parleying after this; the weapon of force is employed, with the issue that we know.

Side by side with this we set the Synoptic account. The general trend of opposition is traceable in St. Mark's Gospel. Jews from Jerusalem appear as murmurers and objectors in the course of the Galilean ministry. The Galilean popularity slips silently away. It is never organized into an effective movement. There is, on the other hand, a highly organized religious system, which feels itself endangered. It is preparing to strike when an occasion may present itself. Our Lord Himself is fully conscious that the visit to Jerusalem which He is about to undertake will end in His death. His forecast, which He repeatedly makes to His disciples, proves to be true. After a few days of public teaching in the temple He is betrayed, arrested, and put to death. But no distinct incidents are emphasised as specially hastening on the crisis. Much is left quite unexplained; as, for example, the sudden enthusiasm of the entry into Jerusalem. The impression conveyed by this part of the narrative in particular is very different from that conveyed by the author of the Fourth Gospel. Our Lord seems to come rapidly from Galilee, pausing briefly at Jericho, where a blind man receives his sight, and then passing on without interruption to Jerusalem. "And when they draw nigh to Jerusalem, at Bethphage and Bethany by the Mount of Olives"—so the somewhat vague description runs—the Lord sends to a neighbouring village for the ass, on which the disciples put their garments, and He sits thereon: "and many strewed their garments in the way, and others branches which they cut from the fields;" and so with shouts of "Hosanna" they conducted Him to Jerusalem. We are left with the idea that our Lord came direct from Jericho to Jerusalem, a distance of about fifteen miles, and that the enthusiasm of His entry was generated in the body of disciples who accompanied Him from Galilee.

To return for a moment at this point to St. John, we find him relating that after the raising of Lazarus Jesus had retired from the neighbourhood of Jerusalem. But presently the passover was approaching, and a week in advance He came back to Bethany, and was present at a supper, at which Mary anointed His feet. It became known that He was there, and people came from the city to see both Him and Lazarus. The next day it was generally known that Jesus was coming to Jerusalem, and, as we have already said, people took palm-branches and came out to meet Him, crying "Hosanna". Then Jesus found an ass and sat thereon, in accordance, as His disciples afterwards remembered, with the ancient prophecy of the King coming to Sion sitting on the foal of an ass. Next follows the incident of the Greeks who sought to see Jesus; and then the general statement of the rejection of the Lord in accordance with the prophecies of Isaiah. After this we have only conversations in private with His disciples until the time of the betrayal and arrest.

I have tried to bring out in strong relief the contrast between the two narratives. Minor inconsistencies there are many; but I cannot feel that, broadly considered, the two accounts are mutually exclusive the one of the other.

The essential difference appears to be a difference of standpoint in telling the story. The one narrator stands in Galilee, so to speak, and watches the fatal progress from Galilee to Jerusalem; the other narrator stands in Jerusalem, or its immediate vicinity, and watches the reception there, and describes the particular circumstances which made it what it was. I am not in the least concerned to maintain that the details of each picture can be so interpreted as to remove what seem to be obvious contradictions. I think that sometimes the historian has to choose between a detail in St. Mark and a detail which conflicts with it in St. John, and that in default of other evidence he must cautiously apply the test of intrinsic probability. I think, for example, that we get from St. John an explanation of the enthusiasm of our Lord's reception which is missing in St. Mark and cannot quite satisfactorily be harmonized with his narrative.

But, when we come to the broad issue, it appears to me to be altogether an exaggeration to say that St. John represents the raising of Lazarus as the immediate cause which led to our Lord's arrest and death. St. John does indeed emphasize in this connection the exasperation and the plotting of His enemies. But he has done this again and again. Let me recall some of the passages. In v. 16, "The Jews persecuted Him, because He had done these things on the sabbath day;" v. 18, "They sought the more to kill Him, because He had not only broken the sabbath, but had said also that God was His own Father, making Himself equal to God;" vii. 1, "He would not walk in Judea because the Jews were seeking to kill Him;" vii. 32, "They sent to take Him;" vii. 44, "Some wished to take Him;" viii. 20, "No man took Him, because His hour was not yet come;" viii. 59, "They took up stones to cast at Him, but Jesus hid Himself and went out of the temple;" x. 39, "They sought again to take Him;" xi. 8, "Rabbi, the Jews were seeking but now to stone Thee, and goest Thou thither again? . . . Thomas said, Let us also go, that we may die with Him." All this is before the raising of Lazarus.

I grant you, if you isolate this section of St. John's narrative, you do get the impression that the raising of Lazarus led to the plots against our Lord's life. But if you come to this incident in its place in St. John's whole story, then you are already supplied with a corrective to such an idea. In proportion as it roused public interest and enthusiasm, it would doubtless whet the edge of hostility; but the intention to destroy Him was already long formed, and already several attempts had been made to carry it out.

3. But, lastly, it is said that if so great a miracle, creating so great a sensation in Jeru-

salem, had actually taken place, St. Mark must have known of it and mentioned it. Now, this is the well-known argument from silence, an argument which historians have again and again found to be misleading. That a writer omits to mention a matter which he might reasonably be expected to mention may admit of various explanations. One explanation, of course, is that no such thing occurred, and therefore he makes no mention of it. But we must be sure that we have exhausted all other alternative explanations before we can adopt this with any sort of security. It has proved a pitfall again and again.

In this particular instance, the argument that St. Mark must have known and referred to the raising of Lazarus, if it really took place, loses half its force when we no longer believe that it was the immediate cause which led to the crucifixion. If all would have gone smoothly but for this, if this was the palpably obvious reason why the attack was then made, it would be difficult to suppose that St. Mark could have omitted to mention it. But if it be true, as all the Gospels indicate, that for some time Jesus had known that His life was in danger, and that Jerusalem would certainly be the place of His death, then the incident loses its special significance in this respect in the general story.

And the force of the argument from silence is still further weakened, if we allow that much, very much, happened in and near Jerusalem which St. Mark does not record. Moreover the whole period now in question is, as we have seen, but briefly treated in his Gospel. His story is hastening to the final scenes; he has already told of one instance of the raising of the dead; he need not tarry to tell another, even if it has reached his ears. He has enough from his Galilean point of view to explain the fatal issue: he has no need to explain, if indeed he knew, that the issue was hastened by the public sensation which this miracle produced.

These, at any rate, are considerations which must be weighed, if we are to do ordinary justice to St. John's narrative. There are others of a more positive kind which, as it seems to me, go to support the credibility of the whole account. Thus, from quite a different source—neither St. Mark nor St. John—comes a brief incident, which throws incidental light on the question, and gives us more than one clue. St. Luke, long before he brings the Lord to Jerusalem for the closing scenes, tells a story about Mary and Martha, two sisters with whom Jesus stayed as a guest. He does not say—perhaps he did not know—where their home was. If it was at Bethany (and there is no reason at all to doubt it), then we have incidental knowledge that our Lord was within two miles of Jerusalem some time, as it would seem, before His final visit. In other words, we have a fresh reason for stretching St. Mark's framework, and for recognizing that he has omitted much that actually occurred.

But what is more important, this brief incident depicts by a few clear strokes the characters of the two sisters: so strikingly, indeed, that their names have become proverbial, the one for impetuous bustle, the other for quiet devotion. Now St. John's story shows us the same two women in a wholly changed situation, plunged in inconsolable grief. The Master's arrival is announced. Mary seems to hear nothing; Martha leaps up and runs to meet Him. Soon she is hurrying back to say, "The Master is come, and is calling for thee". Then Mary comes, and throws herself at His feet. The most minute study of the one incident could hardly have suggested these details of the other. The circumstances are quite different, but we feel that the characters are the same. If we found such a parallel anywhere in historical literature, we should say that it enhanced our confidence in both writers. We should say that the stories were true to life.

The identity of the characters which meet

us in the Synoptic Gospels and then again, in changed situations, in the Fourth Gospel is a subject worthy of careful study. See, for another example, the sudden and overwhelming emotion of St. Peter in St. Luke's story of the miraculous draught of fishes (v. 8). "When Simon Peter saw it, he fell down at Jesus' knees, saying, Depart from me, for I am a sinful man, O Lord". See the same sudden emotion, and the like outburst of exaggerated language, in the totally different scene of the washing of the disciples' feet. "Thou shalt never wash my feet. . . . If I wash thee not, thou hast no part with Me. . . . Lord, not my feet only, but also my hands and my head."

And what shall we say of the central Figure of the Gospels? Is He essentially the same in new situations and confronting different problems? There is, indeed, a great contrast between the language which He holds about Himself; a great contrast, too, between the brief utterances of the Synoptic records and the extended discourses and prolonged disputations of St. John's Gospel. We can do something by consideration of difference of time and place, and something by making allowance for St. John's own strong personality and long intervening experience, to soften and explain the contrast. Yet it remains a difficulty. But when we turn from the speeches to the speaker Himself, we find Him always under the most divergent conditions the same: the same in power to supply all human needs, the same in sympathy for every human misfortune or sorrow, the same in the large liberty which breaks down every conventional barrier that would hamper the full play of His sympathy and His helpfulness. He is as truly man in the Fourth Gospel as in the other three—subject to weariness, hunger, disappointment, sorrow, and pain. He is as plainly more than man in the first three Gospels as in the Fourth, offering to men what no mere man ever offered, claiming from men that absolute surrender to Himself which God alone can rightly claim. Such as He was to the first writers, such He was to St. John: the friend, even the servant, of His disciples; and yet ever and unmistakably their Master and their Lord.

III.

It is not possible within the narrow compass of three lectures to do justice to so large a subject of inquiry as the historical character of the Fourth Gospel. An adequate treatment would require a volume of critical studies. What has seemed possible, and what I have attempted, is the humbler task of a general survey of the problem in the light of modern investigations. My object has been to indicate broadly the difficulties which present themselves when St. John's narrative is compared with the Synoptic narratives, and then to offer some considerations which help to explain the diversity and which certainly ought to be borne in mind before an adverse verdict is recorded. The last thing which a sober historian will do is to abandon a document which has strong external evidence of authenticity. He will try every resource of explanation before he pronounces its narrative of events fictitious. He will be very slow to dispose of what professes to be the account of an eye-witness by the hypothesis that it is an allegorical composition written to inculcate special doctrines. Not that such a form of literature would necessarily be inappropriate as a vehicle of spiritual instruction, or inconsistent with a high view of Biblical inspiration. That is not the point in question. What I say is that the historian must refuse, as long as he reasonably can, to give away one of his principal documents on any such hypothesis. And I cannot think that in the present instance he is reduced to such a policy of despair. The abandonment of even fairly well-attested documents is a perilous path, and the criticism which advances upon it generally has to retrace its steps.

Though I used just now the metaphor of an adverse verdict, it should be remembered that the investigations of history are not really like the proceedings of a court of law. There an issue must be reached and recorded once for all. A witness is examined, cross-examined, and dismissed. The jury decide upon the facts, judgment is given, and the matter is ended. But here we never reach finality. Our verdict is provisional, and the case is tried again and again. The witness with the honest face and the puzzling evidence is always with you, and cannot be dismissed. You may reject his evidence and write your history without him;

but there he is, perpetually protesting against its incompleteness. We have not to win a case which must be decided for practical purposes one way or the other in a brief space of time. We can afford to suspend judgment, if need be, for the sake of fuller investigation. The forged Decretals and the fictitious chronicle of Ingulphus are finally discredited, and will not trouble historians again. But I am confident that we cannot reject half our available evidence, and write a Life of Christ as if the Gospel of St. John had no existence.

The interest of such a question as this is not confined to the circle of critics and historians. Every thoughtful man is concerned to know whether in reading the narratives of the Fourth Gospel he is reading facts or fiction. And therefore it has seemed to me important to offer in plain and untechnical language some serious considerations, which in my judgment make it impossible to dismiss this Gospel as a devout allegory and to proceed to write history without it.

Our limited inquiry can deal with but a few specimens of the difficulties which are urged. Some matters of high interest we must leave aside, such as the omission of any account of the institution of the Lord's Supper, although the spiritual truths which underlie it are expounded and enforced in the conversation which follows St. John's narrative of the feeding of the five thousand; such again as the discrepancy regarding the date of the crucifixion, which St. John appears to place on the day on which the passover lamb was killed, while the Synoptists appear to place it on the following day, thus making the Last Supper coincide with the paschal meal. I mention these examples lest I should be thought to minimize the extent of diversity. On the contrary, I recognise that of these and other difficulties no satisfactory solution has been offered which can be said to meet with general consent.

We shall conclude our brief survey by some remarks on a subject of yet greater interest—the historical value of the narratives which St. John gives us of the appearances of our Lord after His resurrection. We may begin by observing that in the accounts of the four Evangelists at this point we find at once discrepancy in detail and agreement as to the central facts. But why, it may be asked, should discrepancies have been allowed at all at so vital a point of the history? Surely if anything needed to be recorded with precision it was this, which was to be adduced for ever afterwards as testimony to fact.

In answer I would remind you, first of all,

that the early Christians were not dependent in any way on these written narratives for their evidence of the Resurrection. They had seen the Lord—that was enough. Nay, that would of itself throw the first incidents into the shade for the time, only to be reproduced later for the instruction of others. Nor even then would they be offered as proofs: the proof to the new converts would be the living testimony of those who had seen the Lord.

Secondly, the various narratives were set down for instruction as each writer was in a position to tell them. There was no idea that it was important to harmonize them in detail. The Church which accepted the Four Gospels could not have been blind to the obvious superficial discrepancy; it meets every reader at once; it was as plain then as it is now. But the Church accepted them and bound them into one volume, so to speak, as furnishing together a true general picture of the events of that stirring time. This was, indeed, the greatest service that could be rendered to the future; for instead of having four guaranteed accounts, manipulated by an early criticism and shorn of their distinctive features, we have four voices speaking to us out of the past, and reproducing much of the confusedness which history again and again discovers in the earliest accounts of very startling and overwhelming events. We sometimes hear it alleged against the early Christian writers that they were not critical in their methods. It is this very fact which has left us simple narratives which we can set side by side and compare. It has made criticism possible for us. If we cannot reconstruct the whole series of events and fit everything into place, we can do what is most important—get behind the variations and discern the more confidently the points of common agreement.

The most striking of all the divergences relates to the localities in which our Lord showed Himself to His disciples. St. Mark's narrative clearly points to Galilee as the meeting-place. It represents the Lord as saying before His crucifixion, "After that I am risen, I will go before you into Galilee". When Mary Magdalen and the other women come to the tomb, they find the stone rolled away, and a young man in a white robe sitting inside, who says, "He is risen, He is not here: behold the place where they laid Him: but go and say to His disciples and Peter, He goeth before you into Galilee: there ye shall see Him as He said unto you". St. Mark's Gospel breaks off abruptly almost immediately after this, in the middle of a sentence, the last leaf having been lost at an early period. But no one can reasonably doubt that it went on to describe the fulfilment of the twice-repeated promise of an appearance to the disciples in Galilee. Thus we have a feature of St. Mark which is wholly characteristic—the restriction of interest to Galilee. Galilee to him had been the centre of the Lord's activity; Jerusalem was the scene of suffering, visited that He might die there; Galilee was again to be the scene of renewed activity. What limited his interest thus we may never fully know, but the fact is there.

St. Matthew's Gospel, the writer of which was using St. Mark and possibly had the last leaf which now is missing, goes on to narrate an appearance of the Lord to these same women, and then subsequently the promised appearance in Galilee. St. Luke, on the other hand, has no special interest in Galilee, and he has other sources of information which tell him of appearances in Jerusalem. He therefore does not give the promise that there will be an appearance in Galilee, though he has St. Mark before him at this point. It is possible that he had not the last leaf, and did not know of any Galilean incident to relate. However this may be, he passes on to tell the story of two who went to Emmaus, to whom the Lord revealed Himself, and then he tells of the appearance to the disciples the same night in Jerusalem. But his narrative never brings our Lord to Galilee again.

When we turn to St. John we find a number of incidents told in his own peculiar way, with many details that are fresh to us, and some which we cannot quite harmonize with the parallel accounts. But we find that he bears out St. Mark by recording an appearance in Galilee —that he bears out St. Matthew both in this respect and also in so far as he records a first appearance to one at least of the women, St. Mary Magdalen—and that he bears out St. Luke by recording an appearance to the disciples on the first night in Jerusalem. So that from the point of view of locality we find St. John giving a general confirmation to the sum of the other narratives.

Let us now glance at some other agreements.

1. All the narratives agree that on the morning of the first day of the week the stone was found rolled away from the tomb, and the body of Jesus was not there.

2. All the narratives agree in giving no description at all of the act of resurrection, or of the emerging of the Lord from the tomb. This restrained truthfulness may be contrasted with the fanciful description contained in the apocryphal Gospel of Peter.

3. All agree in representing the Resurrection

as a complete surprise, though all agree in recording that our Lord had foretold it more than once to His disciples.

4. All agree in recording no appearance of any kind to His adversaries. There was no attempt to force conviction upon the unwilling and the hostile. The revelation of the Lord was made only to loving and devoted disciples.

5. Once more, St. John agrees with St. Luke, whose account is the next to his in fulness of detail, in making it plain that the Resurrection was no mere revival, no return to the old conditions and limitations of our ordinary life. In St. Luke the Lord is not recognised by the two disciples on the way to Emmaus, although He holds much converse with them, until He chooses to make Himself known; and then He suddenly vanishes out of their sight. When they have hurriedly returned to Jerusalem, they are met with the news that the Lord has been seen by St. Peter; and, while they are telling their tale, suddenly the Lord, who had left them at Emmaus, is seen standing in their midst. In St. John we gain the impression that the sacred body was withdrawn from the wrappings of the grave-clothes without seriously disturbing them. We find that Mary Magdalen fails to recognise the Lord until He addresses her by name; that He suddenly appears to His disciples when the

doors are shut and barred for fear of the Jews; and that as He stands upon the shore of the Lake of Galilee the disciples do not recognise Him until the beloved disciple whispers to Peter, "It is the Lord". Both of these evangelists incidentally suggest to us that the Resurrection of Christ was an act belonging to the spiritual order, transcending and controlling the material. It was thus a pledge and a promise of the resurrection of Christians, when, according to the great saying of St. Paul, this corruptible shall have put on incorruptibility, and this mortal immortality. Yet no such interpretation is definitely offered by either evangelist: only the acts are recorded from which such an inference may be drawn.

From this comparative analysis we may pass on to consider what it is that St. John actually records for us. To begin with his narrative of the burial, he says in agreement with St. Mark that the sacred body was asked from Pilate by Joseph of Arimathea. He describes him as "a disciple of Jesus, but in secret for fear of the Jews". St. Mark says that he was a "counsellor of repute" (*i.e.*, a member of the Jewish Sanhedrin), but he adds "who himself also was looking for the kingdom of God". The two descriptions supplement each other, and are equally applicable to Nicodemus, who, as St.

John tells us, accompanied Joseph, bringing a rich gift of spices for the hasty burial. If we suppose that the little company of women watched their proceedings from some distance, we need find no inconsistency here with the statements of St. Mark that "they beheld where He was laid," and yet themselves bought spices for His anointing as soon as the Sabbath was past.

Early on the first day of the week, St. John tells us, Mary Magdalen came in the darkness to the garden, and saw that the stone was taken away from the tomb. The tomb, according to St. Mark, must have been of considerable size, for he not only speaks of the women as entering and coming out, but he also speaks of the door or doorway of the tomb. St. John's language in the original may be compared with that which he uses at the raising of Lazarus, "Take away the stone"; and it presents no difficulty if we conceive of the great stone as having been at least partially thrust into the doorway. I mention this detail, because a point of discrepancy has been suggested, without, I think, sufficient reason.

Mary Magdalen sees nothing more than that the stone is out of its place. She concludes that some one has come and taken the body away; and she runs at once to St. Peter and the other disciple, whom we are accustomed to identify with St. John, and tells them, "They have taken the Lord out of the sepulchre, and we know not where they have laid Him". It is interesting to note in passing the plural, "we know not," which suggests what St. John has not mentioned—that there were others who shared her anxiety. Peter and John run to the tomb; John, the younger man, is the first to arrive; he looks in and sees the linen cloths in their place (the words in the original are curiously emphatic—*βλέπει κείμενα τὰ ὀθόνια*). Peter, when he comes, enters the sepulchre; he too observes the linen cloths in place, and he sees also that the napkin which had been bound round the head was not in place; it was still rolled up, but fallen aside. This strange description would be accounted for if we suppose a change to have passed over the body, releasing it from material limitations, so that it could be withdrawn without unwinding its wrappings. But no such interpretation is offered by the evangelist, who simply tells that he also entered, and saw and believed. It was the first dawn of his faith; for none of them, he tells us, had as yet understood from the Scriptures that the Resurrection must necessarily take place.

Next, with no definite note of time, we find Mary Magdalen standing by the sepulchre outside and weeping. Then she looks in and sees two angels, "one at the head and the other at the feet, where the body of Jesus had lain". Presently turning back she sees, but does not recognise, the Lord Himself. He reveals Himself to her by calling her by her name. Late in the evening of the same day Jesus stands in the midst of the disciples when the doors were shut, and charges them with a mission like His own, and endows them with a gift of the Holy Spirit for its fulfilment. Thomas was absent, and he refused to believe until he should have the assurance of his own sight and touch. A week later the Lord appeared again in their midst, and offered Thomas the very evidence which he had demanded. The sight of the Lord was enough, and Thomas exclaimed, "My Lord and my God". With this climax of faith the evangelist brings his Gospel to a formal close. "Many more signs indeed Jesus did in the presence of His disciples which are not written in this book. These have been written that ye may believe that Jesus is the Christ, the Son of God, and that believing ye may have life in His name."

What is there here that raises any fresh difficulty from the historical point of view? Is there anything which should suggest to us that St. John's narrative has less historical probability than that of St. Luke? It is true that St. John speaks of Mary Magdalen alone, while St. Mark speaks of two other women as coming with her to the tomb; and, further, St. John says nothing of the appearance of the young man in a white robe who gives a message for the disciples to the women. When carefully compared the two accounts are not necessarily inconsistent, but we need not stay to prove this. If so be that they cannot be quite made to fit into each other, it does not follow that either one or the other is untrue; and there is no ground for specially rejecting that which is given by St. John.

But there is one assumption which, if it is justified, entirely discredits St. John's narrative. I mean the assumption that there were no appearances of the Lord in Jerusalem at all, or, at any rate, none until after the disciples had been to Galilee and returned again. But it is hard to treat this assumption seriously, for it directly contradicts the evidence of each of the four Gospels. St. Mark does not relate any appearance of the Lord at all, because his Gospel breaks off suddenly, as we have seen. He points to a forthcoming appearance in Galilee, but his language plainly implies that the disciples were still at Jerusalem, whereas the assumption to which we have referred rests on the belief that the disciples fled in terror at once from Jerusalem to Galilee. St. Matthew —continuing St. Mark's broken account, it would seem—relates that our Lord met the women on their way from the sepulchre. St. Luke gives a full account of two appearances on the first day of the week—the one in the vicinity of Jerusalem, the other in the city itself. Unless we reject the testimony, direct or indirect, of all our earliest documents, we cannot suppose that the appearances of our Lord were confined to Galilee.

We have seen that St. John formally closes his Gospel with the supreme instance of the faith of St. Thomas. He returns to his task, however, to narrate one more incident. The old apostle had lingered when all who had known the Lord on earth were gone. It was thought that he would tarry till the Lord returned; it was even believed that the Lord had so declared. To the group of his faithful disciples he explained the facts; and so we have gained, by way of an appendix, one of the most beautiful of all the Gospel stories, the appearance of the Lord by the Sea of Galilee, and the restoration of St. Peter. Its conclusion gives the motive of the narrative, and then those who have drawn the story from him add their own witness to the truthfulness of what he has written: "Jesus said not to him that he should not die, but, If

I will that he tarry till I come, what is that to thee? This is the disciple that beareth witness concerning these things, and hath written these things; and we know that his witness is true."

It was their personal knowledge of the writer that drew from these his disciples their spontaneous witness to his truthfulness. The lack of such personal knowledge is supplied for us to some extent by the character of the writer as it reveals itself in his writings. With this thought I must conclude what I feel to be a very imperfect survey of a difficult and much controverted subject. I would not claim to have done more than show that some grave difficulties are much diminished when we attend carefully to the evangelist's own indications of his purpose and method, and that some facts which we owe to him alone supply a gap in our knowledge with a very high degree of historical probability. My chief aim has been to remove the preliminary distrust with which the student of the synoptic records is apt to approach the Fourth Gospel, and to suggest to him that the historical character of its narrative will stand out more and more convincingly as it is reverently and patiently investigated. In other words, St. John will justify himself to us, if we will become his disciples. The more closely we study his book, and the more sympathetically we yield ourselves to his instruction, the more shall we appreciate both the simplicity of his narrative and the profundity of his interpretation of the life of the Lord, and the more readily shall we echo the naïve words of that early confirmation of his narrative, "We know that his witness is true".

NOTE.—ON THE ALLEGED MARTYRDOM OF ST. JOHN THE APOSTLE.

In the foregoing lectures I have not dealt with the problem of the authorship of the Fourth Gospel, as I had nothing to add to what I said in an earlier lecture, now published in *The Study of the Gospels* (Longmans, 1902). On one point of detail which bears on this problem, however, a good deal of discussion has recently taken place —namely, the manner of the Apostle's death. In the lecture referred to I said (p. 151):

> The prevailing tradition of the Church is that which is preserved by Irenaeus, a disciple of Polycarp of Smyrna, who in turn had been acquainted with St. John. It is to the effect that the Apostle lived to a great age, and died at Ephesus in the closing years of the century. A single voice is raised in contradiction of this tradition. It is a supposed statement of Papias in his second book of *Expositions*, preserved in two late chroniclers, to the effect that "John the Divine and James his brother were put to death by the Jews". Papias himself of course could not have used the epithet "the Divine" (*ὁ θεολόγος*). If he merely said "John and James" it is probable that he referred to the Baptist, and that a false identification

with the Apostle was made in later times. This is Dr. Zahn's explanation. Lightfoot and Harnack offer a less simple solution, but agree in dismissing the notice as of no historical value. Irenaeus and Eusebius knew the work of Papias, and yet maintained with no shadow of a doubt the universal tradition of St. John's peaceful death in old age. It may further be noted that, whoever may be regarded as the author of the last chapter of the Fourth Gospel, it is clear that he believed that St. John "tarried" after the rest of the apostolic band had passed away.

I take this opportunity of dealing with the problem more fully, especially as a fresh contribution to the subject has been made by Dr. J. H. Bernard, the Dean of St. Patrick's, in the first number of the *Irish Church Quarterly* (January, 1908). Dr. Bernard discusses the language of the alleged statement of Papias, and also the significance of the position of St. John's Day in the ecclesiastical calendars. In regard to the second of these points in particular I shall follow him, with some slight modifications and amplifications of his argument.

1. *The alleged statement of Papias.* The authority for this statement is an Oxford MS. (Bodl., *Baroccianus*, 142), which probably represents an eighth or ninth century Epitome of the History of Philippus Sidetes (cent. v.). The statement is as follows:

Papias, Bishop of Hierapolis, who was a hearer of John the Divine and a companion of Polycarp, wrote five books of Oracles of the Lord, in which, etc. . . . Papias in the second book says that John the Divine and James his brother were killed by the Jews.[1]

We may note, first of all, that the writer of this passage betrays carelessness in speaking of Papias as having written "Oracles of the Lord," the well-known title of his book being *Expositions of the Oracles of the Lord.* We shall not therefore be surprised if we find that he has misquoted or misinterpreted Papias's words at this point, whatever they may have been.

[1] Παπίας Ἱεραπόλεως ἐπίσκοπος, ἀκουστὴς τοῦ θεολόγου Ἰωάννου γενόμενος, Πολυκάρπου δὲ ἑταῖρος, πέντε λόγους κυριακῶν λογίων ἔγραψεν, ἐν οἷς κ.τ.λ. . . . Παπίας ἐν τῷ δευτέρῳ λόγῳ λέγει ὅτι Ἰωάννης ὁ θεολόγος καὶ Ἰάκωβος ὁ ἀδελφὸς αὐτοῦ ὑπὸ Ἰουδαίων ἀνῃρέθησαν (De Boor, *Texte u. Unters.*, v, 2, 170). Into one of the MSS. of the *Chronicon* of Georgius Monachus an interpolator has inserted a similar statement, which however contradicts the whole of the original context of Georgius: [Ἰωάννης] μαρτυρίου κατηξίωται (instead of ἐν εἰρήνῃ ἀνεπαύσατο). Παπίας γὰρ ὁ Ἱεραπόλεως ἐπίσκοπος, αὐτόπτης τούτου γενόμενος, ἐν τῷ δευτέρῳ λόγῳ τῶν κυριακῶν λογίων φάσκει ὅτι ὑπὸ Ἰουδαίων ἀνῃρέθη· κ.τ.λ. That this is taken from the epitomiser of Philippus Sidetes, and not directly from Papias, is in itself probable, and is almost conclusively proved by (1) the careless description of Papias's work as κυριακὰ λόγια, instead of κυριακῶν λογίων ἐξηγήσεις, and (2) the unusual reference ἐν τῷ δευτέρῳ λόγῳ, instead of ἐν τῷ δευτέρῳ βιβλίῳ, which is the regular use in quoting from Papias. This second statement is accordingly of no independent value.

Secondly, in giving to St. John the title of "the Divine," he shows that he cannot be quoting Papias *verbatim*. He has added the epithet himself, to define which "John" he considers Papias to mean. It is possible that the definition "his brother" may also be a supplement added to define which "James" is meant. Papias may have simply said, "John and James were killed by the Jews". If we found such a statement in an early writer, we should probably interpret it either of John the Baptist and James the son of Zebedee, who were put to death by the two Herods; or of John the Baptist and James the Lord's brother, the latter of whom notoriously was killed by the Jews.[1]

Whether the explanation here suggested be the true one or not, is of no very great importance. What is important is the question whether the statement that St. John the Apostle was killed by the Jews can reasonably

[1] Dr. Bernard points out that the very expression ὑπὸ Ἰουδαίων ἀνῃρέθη was almost certainly employed by Eusebius in recording the death of James the Lord's brother in his *Chronicle*, the Greek of which has to be reconstructed from the Latin and Armenian versions. The fact of his murder by the Jews is of course well known from Josephus and Hegesippus, and it was commonly regarded as one of the special crimes which led to the Divine vengeance upon Jerusalem.

be attributed to Papias, who if he had not actually been a hearer of the Apostle, as Irenaeus tells us he was, yet certainly was the friend of Polycarp who was St. John's disciple. On this point Harnack says (*Chronologie*, i, 665 f.):

> How are we to believe that such a statement can come from the second century, and can have stood in a work which was read by Irenaeus, Eusebius and many others? Could they all alike have passed it over in silence? And, besides, must John xxi count for nothing, a passage which plainly presupposes the death of John, but—in contrast with that of Peter—not his death by martyrdom?

Harnack accordingly rejects the statement as unhistorical, and he offers a somewhat elaborate theory to account for the mistake made in attributing it to Papias. Without committing ourselves to this or any other theory of explanation, we may accept his verdict that the general tradition of the second century, which assigns to St. John the Apostle a peaceful end, cannot be set aside by this slender evidence for a martyr's death.

2. *Supposed corroboration from ecclesiastical calendars.* The position which St. John the Apostle holds in our own calendar is remarkable. On the three days after Christmas we commemorate in turn St. Stephen, St. John, and the Holy Innocents. We are familiar with the popular explanation: the first was a martyr in will and

in deed; the second in will, but not in deed; the last were martyrs in deed, but not in will. This fanciful interpretation illustrates the difficulty which has been felt as to the position held by the festival of the Apostle. Now though the festival of Holy Innocents does not appear till the fifth century, and then only in the West, St. Stephen and St. John have held their respective positions in both East and West from the latter part of the fourth century at least. May we accept the suggestion, which appears to have been made independently by more than one writer, that St. John's position next to the first martyr, St. Stephen, corroborates the otherwise isolated statement that he died a martyr's death? Let us look into the evidence.

A very ancient Syriac martyrology, contained in a MS. which bears the date A.D. 411-412, gives us the following:

> The names of our lords the martyrs and victors, and their days on which they gained (their) crowns . . .
>
> In the month Kanun the first,
>
> Dec. 26. On the xxvith according to the Greeks, the first martyr at Jerusalem, Stephen the apostle, the head of the martyrs.
>
> 27. and on the xxviith, John and James the apostles at Jerusalem.
>
> 28. and on the xxviiith, in the first Kanun, in the town of Rome Paul the apostle and Simon Cephas the head of the apostles of our Lord.

About a hundred years later we have a Carthaginian martyrology,[1] which contains the following:

Dec. 25. viii Kal. Jan. Domini nostri Jesu Christi, filii Dei.
26. vii Kal. Jan. sancti Stefani primi martyris.
27. vi Kal. Jan. sancti Johannis Baptistae, et Jacobi Apostoli, quem Herodes occidit.
28. v Kal. Jan. Sanctorum Infantum, quos Herodes occidit.

The writer of this MS. has changed John the Apostle into John the Baptist, perhaps because he held the common view of the Apostle's peaceful death; but he betrays himself by the fact that he also gives John the Baptist on June 24. There can be no doubt that St. John the Apostle originally stood in this place.

The question then is, Did St. John the Apostle acquire this place in the calendar on the ground that he was believed to have been a martyr? If the question be answered in the affirmative, we may still point to the wider use of the word "martyr," current in the first and second centuries, which included those who had faithfully endured persecution and had survived their sufferings: we may also recall the statement in the Apocalypse that St. John was an exile at

[1] This and the previous martyrology are conveniently accessible in *The Three Oldest Martyrologies*, edited by Lietzmann (Cambridge : Deighton and Bell, 1904, price 6d.).

Patmos "for the witness (the word in the Greek is the same as that used for 'martyrdom') of Jesus"; and also our Lord's prediction that both John and James should "drink of His cup and be baptized with His baptism".

But Dr. Bernard has been able to answer the question in the negative, by going back to yet earlier evidence.

In the first place Dr. Bernard sets side by side with the Syriac martyrology a passage from a Syriac homily *On Persecution* written by Aphrahat in A. D. 344. Aphrahat deals at great length with the sufferings of Old Testament saints, and towards the close he sums up thus:

> Hear, my beloved, these names of martyrs, of confessors and of the persecuted. [Abel, Moses, David, Daniel, etc., are again summarily referred to, and he continues,] Great and excellent is the martyrdom of Jesus. He surpassed in affliction and in confession all who were before or after. And after Him was the faithful martyr Stephen whom the Jews stoned. Simon (Peter) also and Paul were perfect martyrs. And James and John walked in the footsteps of their Master Christ. Also (others) of the Apostles thereafter in divers places confessed and proved true martyrs. And also concerning our brethren who are in the West, in the days of Diocletian there came great affliction and persecution to the whole Church of God, which was in all their region. . . . [1]

[1] *Library of Nicene and Post-Nicene Fathers*, xiii, 401 (Dr. Gwynn's translation). Attention has already been called to this passage by Bousset (see H. L. Jackson, *The Fourth Gospel*, 1906, p. 211).

Here we observe that the same five notable saints are mentioned as in the Syriac martyrology, St. Stephen holding here as there the first place. The coincidence is the more striking in view of the fact that no other New Testament name occurs in the Syriac martyrology, which for the rest consists of local commemorations. It is plain that Stephen, Peter and Paul, and John and James were held in exceptional honour as representative names of the apostolic Church. But does Aphrahat select them on the ground of martyrdom in the strict sense of the word? Plainly not: for in his Old Testament list the majority of those whom he mentions were not persecuted to the death; he speaks of a wider class—"of martyrs, of confessors, and of the persecuted". Moreover, whereas he describes Stephen, Peter and Paul as "martyrs," he is careful to use another phrase in regard to John and James, doubtless because, though James was a "martyr," John in the strict sense was not.

The pre-eminence of these five great names, as the representative saints of the New Testament, receives a remarkable illustration from a passage of Gregory of Nazianzus, to which Dr. Bernard has called my attention since his article was written. Gregory's famous panegyric on St. Basil the Great († 1 Jan. 379) was delivered not long after his return from Constantinople in June 381. Possibly it was spoken on the anniversary of his death in 382. Towards the close of his discourse he says:[1]

> Come then, there have been many men of old days illustrious for piety, as lawgivers, generals, prophets, teachers, and men brave to the shedding of blood. Let us compare our prelate with them, and thus recognise his merit. [Adam, Enos, Enoch, Noah, Abraham, Isaac, Jacob, Joseph, Job, Moses, Aaron, Joshua, Samuel, David, Solomon, Elijah, Elisha, the Three Children, Jonah, Daniel, the seven Maccabees, are passed in review, and the orator continues,] I now turn to the New Testament, and comparing his life with those who are here illustrious, I shall find in the teachers a source of honour for their disciple. Who was the forerunner of Jesus? John, the voice of the Word, . . . [Then he proceeds,] he emulated the zeal of Peter, the intensity of Paul, . . . the lofty utterance of the sons of Zebedee, the frugality and simplicity of all the disciples. . . . He was prevented from becoming a Stephen, eager though he was, since reverence stayed the hands of those who would have stoned him.[2]

There is here a close parallel with the discourse of Aphrahat, both in the long list of Old Testament saints, and in the absence of any names of Christian saints except the five great leaders.

§ 70, I quote the translation given in the *Library of Nicene and Post-Nicene Fathers*, vii, 419.

[2] *Ἐμιμήσατο Πέτρου τὸν ζῆλον, Παύλου τὸν τόνον, τῶν ὀνομαστῶν καὶ μετωνομασμένων ἀμφοτέρων τὴν πίστιν· τῶν υἱῶν Ζεβεδαίου τὸ μεγαλόφωνον· πάντων τῶν μαθητῶν τὸ εὐτελὲς καὶ ἀπέριττον . . . Στέφανος μὲν γὰρ ἐκωλύθη γενέσθαι, εἰ καὶ πρόθυμος ἦν, ἐπισχὼν αἰδοῖ τοὺς λιθάζοντας.*

Basil was not a martyr: therefore Stephen, who cannot be left out, comes in at the end with a word of explanation. It is clear that Peter, Paul, James and John do not owe their preeminence to death by martyrdom.

The next source of evidence to which Dr. Bernard has pointed is the Sermons of Gregory of Nyssa. Following the lead of Duchesne, he refers to an oration in which Gregory commemorates his brother Basil. It is not, I think, right to say with Duchesne that this oration was a funeral oration delivered on the occasion of Basil's death in 379. The passage with which it opens shows that it was spoken on some anniversary of his death, after his commemoration had become a fixed event; and the detachment with which he can speak of the great master would lead us to assign a considerably later date: Gregory did not die before A.D. 395.

The Oration opens thus:

> An excellent order hath God appointed for these our annual festivals, which during these days we have been and still are celebrating in a duly constituted sequence. The order of these our spiritual commemorations is that which we are taught also by St. Paul, whose wisdom in these matters came from above. For he says that in the first place are set the apostles and the prophets, and after them the pastors and teachers. With this sequence of the apostle the order of the year's commemorations

coincides. The first, I do not reckon with the others: for the grace of the theophany of the only-begotten Son, which is manifested to the world through the Virgin-birth, is not simply a holy festival, but the holy of holies, and the festival of festivals. Let us reckon then those which follow this. First of all, apostles and prophets lead the spiritual procession: for the two kinds of gifts belong to the same persons, the apostolic spirit, to wit, and the spirit of prophecy. And the persons are these; Stephen, Peter, James, John, Paul. Then after these, observing his own order, the pastor and teacher introduces our present festivity. And who is he? Shall I tell his name? etc.

He goes on to say that "the pastor and teacher" is Basil, a man worthy to come next after Paul, though so far removed in point of time. It is clear from this passage that immediately after Christmas came the commemorations of Stephen, Peter, James, John and Paul; and then soon afterwards (*i.e.* on 1 January) followed the commemoration of Basil, who had died on 1 January 379. It is clear, too, that to Gregory's mind the first group were thus honoured not as martyrs, but as leaders of the prophetic and apostolic order of the earliest days. Basil, he says, may rightly be commemorated after them; as "the pastor and teacher" properly follows after "the apostles and the prophets". This is rhetoric, of course; and if the passage stood alone it would not be possible to lay much stress on Gregory's opinion, though the facts he alludes to are in any case important.

Dr. Bernard has, however, called attention to another sermon of Gregory of Nyssa, preached on the day after St. Stephen's Day; and from this we may quote some sentences. It begins thus:

> Christ came into the world unto salvation; and after Him sprang up the fruits of the Church. The Witness of the truth shone forth, and there shone forth with Him the witnesses of the great dispensation.[1] The disciples followed the Master, treading in the steps of the Lord. After Christ the Christ-bearers; after the Sun of righteousness the lights of the world. And first we have Stephen[2] flowering forth. [A praise of St. Stephen follows, and the preacher continues,] For it is needful that we should thus in passing pay the protomartyr his due (which yesterday the weakness of the flesh forbade us to render), and then go on to-day to fulfil the appropriate commemoration of the holy Apostles. [He then justifies the linking of these commemorations by saying:] Neither are martyrs without apostles, nor apostles without martyrs; for apostles are the teachers of martyrs, and martyrs the reflections of apostles.

This passage makes it evident that Gregory does not regard the commemoration of the Apostles at this point in the calendar as grounded

[1] In the Greek the same word signifies "witness" and "martyr".

[2] A play on στέφανος "a garland" or "crown of flowers".

on their death by martyrdom. Later he says, in the words quoted by Dr. Bernard:

> To this Stephen all the precious stones (*sc.* of the spiritual temple) were immediately joined together—the most divine heralds of the Gospels; after them the martyrs; and after them again those who have shone with saving virtue—principally those commemorated at this present season, who flash forth the beauty of piety far and brightly, I mean Peter and James and John, the leaders of the apostolic harmony and the crowns of the Church's glory.

These "crowns," he adds, fitly follow Stephen ("the crown"). They have obtained in various ways the honour of martyrdom: Peter crucified head downwards, James beheaded, John suffering divers trials and so being reckoned with the martyrs; "for to those who judge aright martyrdom is determined not by the issue of the suffering, but by the will and desire". It is thus abundantly clear that in St. Gregory's view the Apostles are commemorated at this point as "the divine heralds of the Gospels". That they were also all of them in some sense "martyrs" is added as a further justification of their being linked with St. Stephen.

There is yet another sermon of St. Gregory of Nyssa, which refers to this same collocation of festivals. It was preached on St. Stephen's Day, and begins thus:

How excellent is the sequence of good things, how sweet the succession of gladness! Feast after feast, and grace for grace do we receive. Yesterday we were feasted by the Lord of all, to-day by the imitator of the Lord.

In telling the story of St. Stephen he says that, when the Church grew in numbers,

Stephen was summoned to the aid of the Apostles. And let no man suppose from the name of ministry (or "diaconate") that he held a second rank as compared with the apostolic dignity; for Paul too regards himself as a minister (or "deacon") of the mysteries of Christ; and the Lord of all . . . was as one that ministereth.

He goes on to indicate with admirable discernment the importance of St. Stephen's work as opening a wider door to the message of the Apostles. In the light of the other discourses we may understand him to be justifying, though he does not expressly say so, the position of St. Stephen's festival in relation to the festivals of Apostles which followed.

In view of this evidence from the fourth century—derived from Aphrahat and the two Gregories—as to the collocation of Stephen, Peter and Paul, James and John, it can hardly be maintained that the position of their commemorations in the early calendars is due to a belief that they all suffered martyrdom. Martyrs they were, without exception, in the widest and earliest sense, as Jesus Christ was Himself "the faithful Witness"; and so their inclusion in a martyrology, as indeed the inclusion of the Christmas festival, was capable of justification. But we can no more argue that St. John was a "martyr" in the restricted sense from his inclusion in this group of five which is led by St. Stephen, than we can argue that St. Stephen was an "Apostle" in the restricted sense from his being called an Apostle in the early Syriac martyrology which thus lifts him to the level of the other four.

Our conclusion then is this. There is no sufficient evidence to cast a serious doubt on the universal tradition of the Church that St. John the Apostle died peacefully at Ephesus in extreme old age. The attribution to Papias of the statement that John and his brother James were killed by the Jews rests on very slender authority. It is almost inconceivable that, if Papias really said this, Irenaeus, Eusebius and others who had read Papias should not have referred to it. And it is not difficult to explain the attribution of such a statement to Papias as a mistake due to a careless interpretation.

Nor can this isolated contradiction of the general tradition find any support either in the occasional description of the Apostle as a martyr, or in the position of his commemoration in the calendars of the Church. The word "martyr," which is the common Greek word for a "witness," was not at first restricted to those who had sealed their testimony with their blood. And the collocation of Stephen, Peter, James, John and Paul, as the representative leaders of primitive Christianity, worthy beyond all others to be added to the glorious roll of Old Testament heroes—"the great cloud of witnesses" of the Epistle to the Hebrews—is attested by Christian orators of the fourth century before the date of the earliest extant calendars. Their names *par excellence* represented the Christianity of the New Testament period, and their commemorations followed that of the Lord Himself at the beginning of the Christian year.